MARINES
Saving Lives

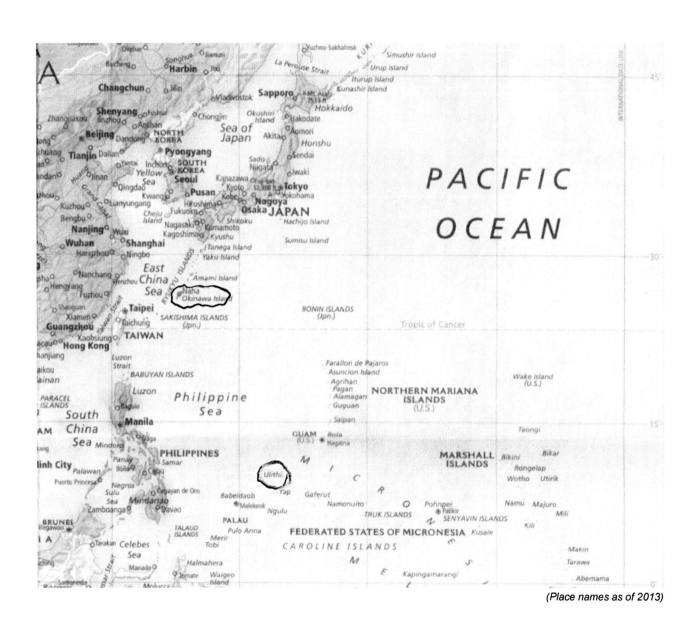

(Place names as of 2013)

MARINES
Saving Lives in WWII:
Semper Fi

by

Bud McDonnell

Kalamazoo Publishing
2013

ISBN 978-0983-1991-6-8

McDonnell, Herbert ("Bud"), 1923–

    Marines saving lives in WWII: Semper fi.
Kalamazoo, Mich.: Kalamazoo Publishing, 2013.

    x, 52 pp.   Includes index, maps, photos

    1. World War 1939–1945—Pacific area—Personal
narrative   2. Naval Aviation Cadet Program   3. Korean
War 1951–1953—United States   4. Marines—United
States—Biography   5. Grayling Air Service (firm)
6. Airports—Michigan—Grayling   7. Real estate
businesses—Michigan—Traverse City   I. Title

940.54 M4788   D790 M4788

Prepublication services:
Words by Design.

CONTENTS

ILLUSTRATIONS

Beechcraft SNB twin-engine trainer planes

PREFACE

After high school, I wanted to be a pilot in World War II and received military training with others to do that. Afterwards we were scheduled to fly the B-25 bomber at Cherry Point, North Carolina, but our orders were changed to San Diego, California, and changed twice again. When I received my Naval Aviation wings, my orders were to fly the R5C (also known as a C-46), a twin-engine Marine transport. Instead of dropping bombs, I become one of many proud Marines who saved hundreds of U.S. Navy ships and perhaps thousands of American lives during the 1945 invasion of the Island of Okinawa about 300 miles south of Japan.

After the war many veterans did not want to talk about it. Because these members of "the greatest generation" are dying at the rate of 1000/day, an urgency exists to record their stories. In December 2003 the Veterans Administration in Battle Creek contacted me and arranged an interview with two high school seniors from Lakeview High School. The VA and the Library of Congress also asked if they could tape our session together to preserve, not only some World War II experiences but also some of the funny things that happened when I was overseas.

I still see and hear both young and older people wanting to know about World War II, so the past few years I have encouraged veterans to write their stores. Margaret von Steinen from Western Michigan University has been holding classes the last three years for veterans at the Portage District Library to help them write their stories. This is my story, finally in written form.

I spent many hours flying two- and four-engine Marine transports across the United States and over the Pacific Ocean, Japan, Korea and China, carrying fellow Marines and supplies. However, what really stands out in my mind was that mission during the invasion of Okinawa which I began to relate in the first paragraph of this Preface.

This was a very difficult mission for the 24 Corsair pilots assigned to it. They had to fly over the ocean in formation off our transport's wings for about 3000 miles—roughly the distance of the U.S. from coast to coast—with only two overnight stops. They could not move around in their cockpits, while our transport crew and few passengers could walk around and had a latrine. This mission saved many U.S. Navy ships and many sailors' lives, and this account of my war-time experiences will tell how I helped save those lives.

In addition, my sons encouraged me to also include my experiences in the Korean War during the 1950s, as well as those of civilian flying after that war. Their interest in aviation and what I could share with them prompted my doing so. Younger members of my family and others are now asking questions about World War II and Korea, so I thought my story may be of interest to your family also.

Bud McDonnell
September 2013

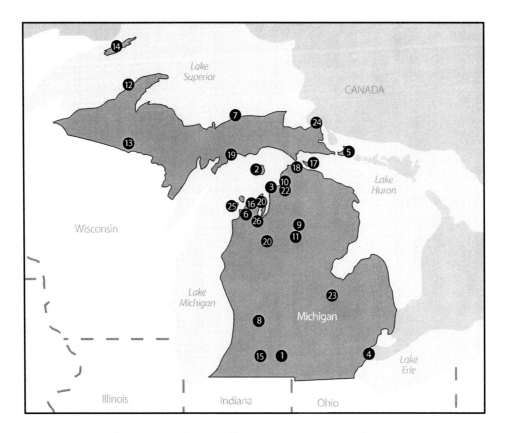

Author's Points of Interest in Michigan

1. Battle Creek
2. Beaver Island
3. Charlevoix
4. Detroit
5. Drummond Island
6. Glen Lake
7. Grand Marais
8. Grand Rapids
9. Grayling

10. Harbor Springs
11. Higgins Lake
12. Houghton-Hancock
13. Iron River
14. Isle Royale
15. Kalamazoo
16. Leland
17. Mackinac Island
18. Mackinaw City

19. Manton
20. Manistique
21. Northport
22. Petosky
23. Saginaw
24. Sault Ste. Marie
25. South Manitou
26. Traverse City

1
GROWING UP

I was born in 1923, the youngest of five children. My first accomplishment was avoiding death when I was a few months old. One day my dad was getting ready to go to work when he told my mother that he was going to check on me. Luckily he did, as I had suffocated. He used mouth-to-mouth resuscitation to get me breathing again. I was not aware of this until I read it in our Bible many years later.

My two brothers, two sisters and I lived with our parents on ten acres at the outskirts of a small town—Grayling, Michigan—in a two-story house. As a young boy I remember the Depression when Mother received the Detroit News and Times every day. It had to be delivered to several households. I met the train from Detroit at 6 a.m., delivered all the papers, and went home before going to school a few miles away.

Our home was very modest, had an outhouse, wood space heater and cooking range, ice box, two large tubs and a hand-wringer for washing clothes, that we hung them up on the clothesline for drying. Our phone was shared with others with an operator. Radio had one station. There was no television. When I got a little older, I worked in a gas station. Gas was twenty cents a gallon. Eventually my dad became postmaster, and we built a new house.

In school I loved sports and hated math. I was very active on the high school basketball and football teams, and was their 6'1" team captain several times. During the last two summers of my high school years, I worked as a trucker's helper in a white uniform with a bright red Coca-Cola insignia on it. The manager often invited me over to his house where I met his sister, Joyce, when she was visiting from the nearby town of Manton.

After Pearl Harbor on December 7, 1941, there was much concern about protecting the Soo Locks from an air attack. So in 1942, the government condemned our ten acres and new home to become part of the new Grayling Army Airfield. I am certain it was a terrible disappointment to Mother and Dad, but they did not complain. They soon would have three sons in the Army and Marine Corps. This proposed airport was never used during the war.

Take the Exam

As not a very good student, I had graduated from Grayling High School in June 1942, and World War II had just started. I went to work for the Coca-Cola Company headquartered in Grand Rapids, Michigan, driving a semi truck, but I wanted to be a pilot, so I paid a visit to the Navy Recruiting Office.

The recruiter informed me that I would have to have at least two years of college when I told him that I had just finished high school. He said, "It is probably a waste of your time," but I could take a written exam that included some math if I wanted to.

Now in retirement, I recently thought of these words, "Take the exam," that seemed to fill the inside of my head and served to shape both my military and civilian lives. In thinking back about it, I recalled how nervous and unprepared I was then, but I was the only guy in the room doing it. Nobody else took it at the same time. To the recruiter's surprise and mine, I passed the exam. Then I had to wait until spring to be assigned to a Navy Flight School as an aviation cadet.

I graduated in June 1944 in Corpus Christi, Texas, receiving my gold naval aviation wings, and was commissioned a Second Lieutenant in the U.S. Marine Corps.

2
NAVAL AVIATION CADET PROGRAM

After passing the written exam for the Naval Aviation Cadet Program, I had to wait until the following March of 1943 before I could be assigned to a base for training. In the meantime, we had to listen to a lecture given by a Naval Aviation officer to all new cadets who may have wanted to enter the Naval Aviation Program during World War II. This is the officer's story as he faced the group and eager eyes looked up at him:

The Lecture

Several men wanting my advice about service careers, had just flattered me with a question about their future. I pondered an appropriate response to a question asked moments earlier. These four bright cadets wanted to know if they should select naval aviation and marine aviation as a career choice.

Finally I said, "Absolutely not. Do not even consider naval or marine aviation. Don't, whatever else you do, go down that path...," I then paused and continued, "unless you have a gracing hunger for excitement, an unquenchable thirst for a challenge, and an eagerness to do things that few men on this planet will have a chance to do. No," I went on, "none of you should start down that path unless you want to experience more excitement in a few

seconds than most people do in a lifetime, unless you want to join a very special organization that is way above other services."

Let me tell you a little bit about naval and marine aviation. I said from the start, you will be pushed to what you think are the limits only to find that there is more in you than you thought. As you begin to learn the basics of flying, both academically and hands-on, the best practitioners of an art that requires very special skills will teach you. They will be both men who have been there and done that. Yes, you will be taught well, but to learn, and learn well, will require a commitment from you, the likes of which you have never known or experienced.

Know this, much will expected from you, but in return, much will be given. You will be taught to rely on your own capabilities and develop self-confidence in your abilities, handle the not-so-routine events, and strive for exactness. You see, aviation, no matter what discipline or service, requires all of these attributes.

Okay, you will make mistakes, you will be expected to, but your instructors and leaders will have done what they could to prepare you, demanding that you acknowledge them and insist that you accept the responsibility for your actions. This is how your predecessors learned and grew. It is how you will learn and grow.

The richness of thousands of experiences will be yours to build upon your knowledge, natural skills and talents. As this process unfolds, you will, without even knowing it, develop a reservoir of knowledge that one day may well mean the difference between a successful flight or becoming a statistic.

You will come to understand that each type of aircraft has its own unique operational envelope, as similarly we each have ours. It might be a dark night, with you as pilot in command, working like the devil to land a cantankerous plane that on a particular night has decided to test you, allowing you only two of the four engines. Your crew of five men and fellow passengers will be depending on your skills to bring them in safely and, as the pilot, you must. It will not matter the crosswinds are out of the limits or that the ceiling and visibility are below minimum. What will matter is that you are the person who is responsible for a safe conclusion to the flight.

The Cadet Program

During the next 16 months I attended five different schools in five different locations. Flight instruction was half a day, and ground school was the other half. I had to work very hard in ground school.

In March 1943, I reported to New Philadelphia, Ohio. We were stationed at its small civilian airport with three flight instructors, and lived in an old house on the airport. We would fly Taylor aircraft which were slightly larger than a Piper Cub.

There were about twenty of us cadets who were issued CCC uniforms that did not fit. The sleeves were about ten inches too short, and the pants about six inches too short, so we wore civilian clothes most of the time. These uniforms came from the Civilian Conservation Corps which had been a public work relief program. It operated 1933–1942 in the United States for unemployed, unmarried men ages 18–25 from relief families (cf., Wikipedia, The Free Encyclopedia).

My first solo, after about eight hours of flight time with the instructor, was a real thrill. The pressure was on not to wash out. If you did wash out or did not solo, in about twelve hours you had orders to Great Lakes Training Center as a Seaman Second Class. This threat remained throughout the Cadet Program.

Practical Military Education

When we cadets finished about 40 hours of flight time and passed all the ground school courses, we then were assigned to a university for extensive ground school training and physical training.

In June 1943, I was transferred to the University of Iowa at Iowa City. We spent a half day studying navigation, meteorology (weather), and Morse Code. We had to be proficient in reading and sending code by radio, blinker lights, and flags. Aircraft engines, aircraft dynamics, aircraft recognition, and military subjects also had to be learned.

The other half day was spent on physical training and marching. This consisted of swimming tests, learning how to survive in the water, running obstacle courses, a lot of time boxing and wrestling, long and short marches, leading troops in platoons and in parades.

It took about three months to pass all the tests before we were assigned to a primary training program. Then we could start flying again.

Training at Naval Air Stations

In October 1943, I was transferred to a naval air station in Hutchinson, Kansas, near Wichita. We flew the Stearman aircraft. It was a two-seat, open cockpit plane, painted yellow. Again, we would fly half days, and have ground school half days. The Stearman was a very rugged aircraft and we had to learn to do snap rolls, loops, spins, and outside loops. Most planes could not stand the stress of outside loops.

Boeing N2S-5 Kaydet

Photo courtesy Kalamazoo Aviation History Museum

Open-cockpit Stearman, Hutchinson, Kansas, Flight School

The most nervous time we had was flying solo at night with eight other planes in the air at the same time. The planes did not have generators, so sometimes the batteries would go dead and someone would be flying around without lights or radios. I also had to get used to taking off and landing in close proximity to other planes.

The airfield did not have runways, but large circular mats. Eight aircraft would takeoff at the same time and return after about two hours of flight time, at the same time. Primary training lasted about three months.

Next stop was basic training. In January 1944, I was transferred to a naval air station in Corpus Christi, Texas. We flew the SNV, a low-wing training plane, with about a 450 horsepower engine, which was very noisy. It was a two-seater place for the student and instructor, and a sliding canopy. After a couple of months I was then transferred to an airfield in Beecville, Texas, to fly the SNV for instrument training.

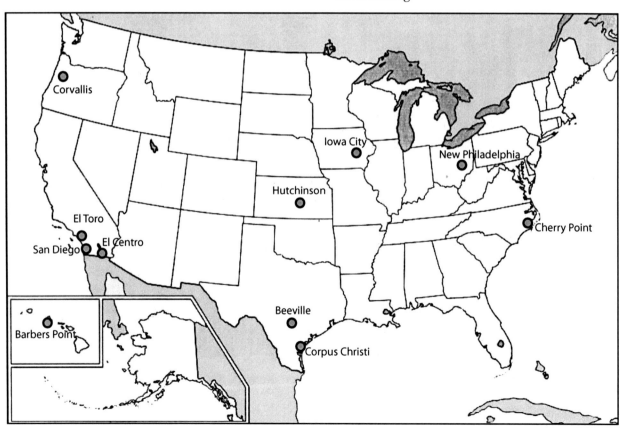

Photo courtesy Squadron Signal Publications, 1993

B-25 Bomber

Decisions to Make

About this time, we were asked to decide whether we wanted to fly twin-engine aircraft or single-engine aircraft. Instructors also needed to know if we wanted to stay in the Navy and graduate as Ensigns or go into the Marine Corps and graduate as Second Lieutenants. I chose the Marine Corps.

Marines were assigned to Cherry Point, North Carolina, to fly the B-25s, a medium bomber. This really appealed to me.

I thought that the Marine Corps would be a much smaller organization—much more efficient than the Navy—and the spirit of the Corps, *semper fi* (always faithful), would be much higher than in the Navy.

In April 1944, I was transferred back to Corpus Christi, Texas, and was assigned to Robb Field for multi-engine training. The plane I flew was a twin-engine Beechcraft SNB. The plane accommodated a pilot, co-pilot, instructor, and three seats with tables for navigation training. Most of the flights were cross-country flights around Texas. The flight cadets would take turns piloting the plane and navigating certain legs of the flight.

Air Sickness

The one time that I came close to being air sick was on one of these flights. It was on a leg where I was doing the navigating. It was a hot summer and we were flying quite low, about 1,500 feet. It was extremely bumpy. I was in the rear seat near the tail and the plane was yawing sideways, plus it being turbulent.

I thought it was a check ride, so I was very nervous. I did not want to make any mistakes estimating times and not giving the correct headings to the check pilot. We landed back in Corpus Christi just at the right time.

Excitement, Disappointment and Blessing

Just prior to graduation in June 1944, receiving my gold wings and Second Lieutenant bars, Joyce and I were married. Instead of orders to Cherry Point to fly B-25s, I had orders to San Diego after about a ten-day leave.

There were about five of us, and we were disappointed and puzzled about going to San Diego. At that time, any Marines going to that city meant you were heading for the Pacific. However, we had received no operational training in combat planes, so we felt it unlikely that we would be sent overseas at that time.

Flying the B-25 would have meant bombing the enemy and causing many casualties. But our orders were changed to pilot the R5C (C-46) twin-engine Marine transport.   Flying the R5C as Corsair escorts, we ended up assisting and saving thousands of American sailors and many U.S. Navy ships.

Pilots flying the Marines' Corsairs (land-based fighter bombers) faced a lot of hardship and danger in flying 3000 miles over the ocean. Engine failure was not uncommon. If men had to ditch into the ocean, their chances of being rescued were very slim. I do not recall any of the Corsair pilots ever mentioning these concerns. They had a job to do.

New Training Sites

When we arrived in San Diego, we were given orders to Corvallis, Oregon, to learn to fly the R4D (C-47) and R5C (C-46) Marine transport planes.

This was an excellent duty and turned out to be very interesting. It was always foggy in the morning, so we did not have to report for duty until about 11 o'clock.

Corvallis was a small town and the home of Oregon State University. The single guys enjoyed it as we were the only servicemen in town with lots of coeds. Joyce came out to join me and we had a small apartment, and a taste of married life.

This did not last long as we were all transferred to El Centro, California. This could be called the armpit of the country. It was in the desert, on the border with Mexico, and not much of a town.

At the airfield the temperatures would sometimes be 110 degrees or higher on the tarmac. Some of the controls in the cockpit would be so hot, we had to wear gloves in order to touch them. There was no air conditioning in those days. At times when we had an early flight, I would have breakfast with Tyrone Power, the famous actor, who was also a Marine pilot.

Welcome to the Pacific Gateway

We were first transferred to the Island of Guam, farther west of Hawaii than Hawaii is from California. In due time, we carried combat Marines and equipment into most of the islands, including Iwo Jima and Okinawa. A friendly rocket hit our landed plane, destroying it in the war's last year. When the war ended, we had orders to fly Marines into Japan and China for the Allied Occupation.

R5C Marine Transport cockpit

Bud with his R5C on Guam

3
GUAM

I was stationed in Guam, a little island in the Pacific, and flying into the Philippines, Peleliu, Ulithi, Kwajalein, Tarawa, Eniwetok, Saipan, and Tinian Islands. The Navy was building up its fleet at Ulithi, southwest of Guam, for the invasion of Iwo Jima and Okinawa.

B-29s were also flying out of Guam, Saipan, and Tinian for strikes on Japan. Iwo Jima was about 700 miles north of Guam and about half-way to Japan, so the island was needed for the damaged B-29s returning from raids on Japan.

Safety First

When I first got overseas, our aircraft carried parachutes for everyone on board. So, before we would takeoff, I would brief the passengers on what could be expected on the flight and the emergency procedures. I instructed them on the life jackets, life rafts, and the use of parachutes. I always thought that if the passengers ever had to bail out, it would have been a time of pure panic.

Soon the squadron received a directive that instructed us to remove the parachutes from the plane except those for the five member crews. Our commanding officer had decided that passengers would be safer, in the event of a serious emergency, not to bail out, but remain in the plane if the pilots had to land in the ocean, as all our flights were over water.

I always briefed the passengers prior to taking off that they were welcome to come up to the cockpit one at a time after we leveled off. They were worried about seeing the parachutes for the crew, but not for the passengers. They would wonder, if the plane got into trouble, was the crew going to bail out and leave them? I assured them that we would never leave them, and it was safer for them to stay with the plane if we did have to ditch it.

The R5C (C-46) that I was flying carried about 30 passengers and was one of the largest two-engine transports at that time. One morning my crew and I were scheduled for a flight to Iwo Jima Island. We loaded the passengers on board, except for one who showed up about a half-hour later, and we started the engines. Our mechanic came up to the cockpit and told us that the passenger had noticed a fluid leak. We shut down the engines so he could investigate the leak. He reported that it was a serious leak; the passengers had to disembark, and the flight was cancelled.

When we took the plane back to our revetment, the leak was determined to be very serious. During the six-hour flight to Iwo Jima, it would have drained all of the hydraulic fluid from the plane. This would have meant one of two things:

1. We would have been unable to lower our landing gear, creating a "wheels up" landing or a crash landing on the Iwo Jima runway, or

2. If we had been able to get the gear down, we would have been unable to have use of the brakes after the landing, a situation even more serious because the runway was not very long. Being unable to stop the plane after the landing was no joking matter.

Part of our R5C squadron on Guam

Bud's R5C crew mates on Guam, 1944

Being Officer of the Day

Housing on Guam consisted of tents. One had a bar and was designated for officers' meals. To relieve ourselves, we just went outside near the tent.

Higher-ups decided to prevent undoubted embarrassment should ever women be visiting by ordering the construction of a more private area. They had a funnel on a tube, raised up two to four feet, put into the ground surrounded by a privacy fence. They called it a pee tube. Orders came down to use it. One day I didn't, and was put "on report."

Everybody took turns being the Officer of the Day. The very next day after being put on report, it was my turn to report to the colonel who thought it was really funny. He was laughing all the while he was chewing me out, but I did have to apologize for not following orders.

Our Squadron's Crucial Assignment

In April 1945, the battle for Okinawa was at its peak.

Four of our R5C (C-46) transport aircraft were to fly east from Guam to Kwajalein Island in the Marshalls and escort 24 Corsairs (F4U), Marine fighter aircraft, to Okinawa by way of Guam and Iwo Jima. Ground forces of Marines had only recently secured Iwo Jima after a bitter battle. On our way back from Okinawa, we were to pick up 30 injured Marines and fly them back to Guam the next day. The full story of this multiple assignment will be told in the following chapters.

Bud and his tent mates on Guam

Iwo Jima from the air

4
IWO JIMA

When Iwo Jima was secured and the runways repaired, we started flying into the island carrying passengers, mail, and whatever was needed. In some of the flights we would carry wounded Marines back to Guam. It took a long time to clean up the island because the Japanese were in caves and tunnels throughout the island. At night the Japanese would come out of the caves and inflict a lot of casualties after the island was so-called "secure." Navy Seabees never received enough credit, as they were in their bulldozers, repairing the runways when the fighting was going on. They were the unsung heroes of the war.

More than 50 years after the war, I had occasion to write this letter to my son:

December 17, 2000

Dear Doug,

I do not recall reading a book about World War II that affected me as much as the book I've just recently read. When Iwo Jima was secured by the Marines, and the Navy Seabees had prepared the airfield runways for landings, our squadron, based in Guam, started flying into the island, delivering supplies and personnel.

I knew that the Marines had a tough time and that we took a lot of casualties, but I was not aware of just how difficult it was. As the author mentions, the 23,000 Japanese troops were all in caves with cement bunkers and were determined not to be taken alive.

On other islands, the Marines could at least see the enemy. On Iwo Jima, they were being shot at and killed from the protected cover of the bunkers. The tanks and other vehicles had difficulty moving because of the deep volcano ash in the area of Mount Suribachi.

At least the taking of Iwo Jima was justified because of the lives that were saved. B-29 crews were saved after making emergency landings on their bombing runs to Japan, and the island provided a base for the invasion of Okinawa as well as the invasion of Japan, which, thank God, did not happen thanks to the BIG bomb.

Dad

Entertainers on Stage and in the Air

A few months after the island was secured, we had orders to fly a U.S.O. troupe (mostly women) to the island to entertain the troops. We had to check into the Iwo Jima tower when we were about 200 miles out. When two of the girls were visiting in the cockpit, I decided to have some fun with the tower operators. I wrote out the message for one of the girls and she called the tower. There was a long silence, and I was told later they could not believe what they heard. Some of the Marines had been overseas two or three years and had not heard a woman's voice except Tokyo Rose.

Tokyo Rose was a generic name given by the Allied Forces in the South Pacific during World War II to any of approximately a dozen English-speaking female broadcasters of Japanese propaganda (cf., Wikipedia, The Free Encyclopedia).

Kamikaze Attack

On one trip to Iwo Jima, we had to remain overnight because of engine problems. After dinner we went out to the plane to have a social drink. Our plane was parked near several B-29s, wing tip to wing tip. I remember it was a moonlit night and the airplanes really shown as they were all silver.

During this time the air raid sirens sounded, and we became quite concerned. Being next to all those planes did not seem too cool. One of our party was an infantry officer, familiar with the island, and he assured us that the Japanese had not bombed the island for sometime, and not to worry; it was probably just a drill. Then we heard the anti-aircraft fire and knew it was no drill. We tried to find some secure places and all we could find was a ridge of gravel about a foot high that the bulldozers had left along the runway.

Things happened pretty fast. The anti-aircraft gunners shot down a two-engine bomber that was heading for our plane and the B-29s. If he had crashed into one, they would have all gone up in flames. Luckily, the gunners hit the wing of the bomber and the plane veered off and crashed about a half a block from us. That was my first experience with a *kamikaze* pilot.

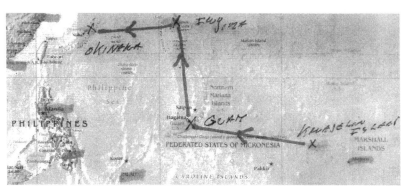

Mission map

5
OKINAWA

This World War II story is about Marine pilots saving hundreds of U.S. Navy ships and perhaps thousands of American lives. It was during the invasion of the island of Okinawa, about 300 miles south of Japan.

In the spring of 1945, our squadron was chosen to escort and navigate for a squadron of F4U Corsair fighter aircraft that was stationed at Eniwetok, an island near the Kwajelein Islands. Both were part of the Marshall Islands 1000 miles east of our Guam base. Our destination was to be Okinawa, which had recently been invaded by the U.S. Marines and the U.S. Army, 1600 miles to the northwest of Guam.

We were flying R5C (C-46) transports, the largest twin-engine transport at that time. Each of our four aircraft was capable of carrying about 30 passengers and was to escort six Corsairs, three on each wing.

Three Corsairs with R5C escort

After picking up the ground crews and aircraft, we took off for Guam, an overnight stay, and then to Iwo Jima, where we again stayed overnight. Up to this point, we had no problems and good weather in escorting the 24 Corsairs.

Things changed when we took off for Okinawa. About half way out, we started running into bad weather. We were then under an overcast, and the navigator was unable to get any sun shots with his sextant. As the clouds became lower, we had to keep descending so that the navigator could read the drift meter. This gave him a measurement of the amount to correct for the wind that was attempting to blow us off course.

As the clouds dropped lower, it became more difficult as we had to remain out of the clouds so that the six planes on our wings could remain in contact with us. Our navigator was becoming very concerned because he was not certain of our exact position. This caused a lot of anxiety as at that time in the war, the Americans had occupied the north half of Okinawa, but the Japanese still had control of the south half.

Finding Yontan Airfield

We had been over water since leaving Iwo Jima, so we had no landmarks. Unfortunately, the first land we saw was very south of the island and we flew over Naha, the largest city, at about 600 feet, just below the clouds. Japanese anti-aircraft guns started firing at us. One of the Corsairs went over on its back, but it rolled out before hitting the ground. We found the Yontan Airfield and all

landed safely. We had to dodge a hazard—some wild horses—on the runway.

The three other transports and their crews in our squadron were to stay overnight at the Yontan Airfield and to return to Guam the next day. That night a Japanese bomber belly-landed on that airfield and blew up our three C-46s (R5Cs). We were told later that several Japanese jumped out of the plane as soon as it stopped by the control tower and ran towards our planes. They placed hand grenades in the landing gear nacelles of the three planes and pulled the pins, setting off an explosion.

We were also told that having the enemy land there was a total surprise causing much confusion, but eventually all of the Japanese were killed. I do not know how many people we lost, but I do know that one of the control tower operators, who was using a spotlight on the Japanese, was killed.

In the short time I was on Okinawa, I learned of the hardship and danger that our Marine and Army ground troops were experiencing fighting the Japanese there. Most of the Japanese were dug into caves that protected them from our artillery and Navy's aerial shells. A great deal of the fighting was done with rifles, mortar fire, hand grenades, and a few tanks. To make matters worse, most of our ground troops had to sleep in their foxholes, and it was raining much of the time.

The battle lasted about three months, from April 1 through end June. I later learned the casualties were high, but I had no idea how high until 2006 when I prepared a report for my church:

Army	5591
Navy	5191
Marines	3263
American civilians	30
Total U.S. casualties	14,005

Three of us in the same Kalamazoo congregation were veterans who served on Okinawa. Most people do not realize the hardship that a lot of veterans experienced, not just getting shot at and losing buddies, but trying to get rest in muddy foxholes. This was not uncommon in the Pacific or Europe during WWII.

Overnight on Ie Shima

After unloading our passengers and refueling at Youtan Airfield, my plane received orders to fly to Ie Shima, a small island off the coast of Okinawa on the Pacific side. The famous war correspondent, Ernie Pyle, was later killed there. Our orders were to stay overnight at Ie Shima and leave the next day for Guam with passengers.

That night we had our own excitement on Ie Shima. The Japanese aircraft (mostly *kamikaze*) had been attacking our Navy ships. Early in the evening, after darkness, we were notified that there was a large Japanese barge with several Japanese on board, heading for us. We were always armed with .45 pistols, but rifles were also issued to us, and our orders were to proceed to the beach where we expected the Japanese to land.

It was pitch black. No lights could be used because of security. We had been given the password to identify other people. It was a very nervous time as we were aviators and not infantry types; we had not trained for being around a lot of people with loaded guns in the dark. I had great respect for the troops who fought on the ground, but this experience showed me the great hardships and the danger to which they were exposed. About midnight, word came that the Japanese had turned back. What a relief!

The next morning our passengers were on board. Many of them were suffering from mental problems, such as battle fatigue, shellshock and other problems from the stress of battle. We were parked about halfway down the runway and just off to the side, keeping our engines running. We were waiting for the "all clear" from the tower before we could takeoff.

A Friendly Rocket Hit

The tower gave three P-47s clearance for takeoff. Then it informed us that we were cleared for takeoff as soon as the P-47s were airborne. I was the only one in the cockpit watching the P-47s taking off. Each plane had three rockets under each wing. As I was watching, one plane started down the runway and a rocket came loose or was fired accidently. It headed directly towards our plane, about two or three feet off the ground.

As before, things happened pretty fast. There was a loud explosion and some of the shrapnel entered the cockpit, but no one was hit. I was the only one in the airplane who knew what had happened. The other members of the crew thought that the Japanese had bombed us. I told everyone that we had been hit by a rocket from the P-47 that had just taken off. The only thing that we could think of was to get out of the plane as soon as possible because we thought the plane would catch fire. Luckily, everyone got out safely. I sprained my ankle when I had to jump from about ten feet.

It was miraculous that no one was badly injured. As we discovered later, the rocket had hit the ground twice before it exploded. If it had exploded upon its first impact, the shrapnel would have hit most of the people in the cockpit and the passenger compartment.

The P-47 pilot returned and landed, and then came over and apologized to us. We assured him

that it was not a nice way for an Army Air Force person to treat us Marines. It was a mechanical error and was certainly not his fault. We then had to wait a few days for one of our planes from Guam to pick us up and return us to base.

Although we left Guam with four C-46s and returned with none, we did get the Corsairs to Okinawa safely. They were badly needed to protect the Navy's loss of many ships from *kamikaze* pilots. Yes, we lost our four Marine R5C (C-46) transports, but how many U.S. Navy ships were saved by the 24 Corsairs and their pilots that we delivered to Okinawa?

We will never know, but we were told that we saved several ships and hundreds of sailors.

Chance Vought F4U/FG1D Corsair

Photo courtesy Kalamazoo Aviation History Museum

Marine Corsairs were land-based aircraft.

6
LIFE AFTER WORLD WAR II

After the war, Mother happily took down her three-star flag from the front window of the house. Her sons and son-in-law were back home safe and sound. I had a new bride and was undecided what to do. I thought seriously about going to college, but deep down I wanted to keep flying. However, it was difficult to get a job as a pilot. The airlines were not hiring many new pilots, and there were a lot of ex-military pilots looking for the few jobs that were available. I thought that aviation had a bright future and was in its infancy, like the automobile after World War I.

I looked at the new unused airfield and thought that it offered an opportunity to Grayling for civilian use as a base for training pilots, charter air services, servicing visiting aircraft, and other aviation uses. I talked my brother, Clayton, into forming the Grayling Air Service to provide these services.

The first thing we did was to go to the meeting of the Grayling City Council and suggest that they take over this exceptional airport. We would then lease space from them for an air service and a flying school. At the time, the City could have purchased the airport for the large sum of one dollar. They felt that the cost of maintaining the airport would

be too great of an expense. They turned down our proposal.

We next visited the Director of Aviation for the State of Michigan. He and his board were in complete agreement with us that the airport should be open to civilian aircraft, but they did not have the financial means to help us.

Our only recourse now was to obtain a lease on a few acres of land near the control tower to build some hangars and have use of the airport for ourselves and the flying public. About this time we paid a visit to the Grayling State Bank, and they informed us that if we could obtain the lease and use of the airport, they would finance us. We began our negotiations with the Corps of Engineers in Chicago. However, in the middle of the negotiations, the Federal Government turned over the jurisdiction of the airport to the War Assets Administration in Detroit. This was very disappointing, to say the least, but after many trips to Detroit, we finally obtained the lease.

We went back to the bank with high hopes that we could now obtain the financing and get on with our plans, but were informed that the bank board had decided that we would need to build the hangars before they would help us. It had taken almost a year to get to this point, and we felt that we could not give up. So Clayton and I erected three hangars, an office and a lounge during the middle of winter with cold wind blowing across the airport. We were turned down again.

Not ones to give up while there was still a chance of succeeding, we then went to banks in Traverse City and Petosky, Michigan, only to be turned down twice more. We were very discouraged at this point, and did not see how we could proceed.

One sunny day we were sitting in front of the hangars and a Navion aircraft landed and taxied up to the gas pumps to be refueled. This pilot must have sensed our depression and asked about our problems. We informed him that we could not obtain the financing that we needed for the air service and flying school. He suggested we try Michigan National Bank in Saginaw, as they had a reputation as a very progressive bank. We mentioned that other out-of-town banks had turned us down, and we saw no point in driving to Saginaw just to be turned down again for a loan. This pilot was very insistent, so Clayton and I decided to give it a try.

In our meeting with the loan officer, he asked what we needed and how much we needed. We told him that we needed three aircraft for training purposes and a line of credit for processing accounts receivables from the Veterans Administration for G.I. flight training as student pilots. He was very receptive. When Clayton and I got up off the floor where we had fallen, he had the documents ready for our signatures.

Bud and son Doug find an extant R5C at the Oshkosh, Wisconsin, EAA fly-In

7
GRAYLING AIR SERVICE

We had a four-place Seabee amphibian aircraft that could land and takeoff on water. One time I picked up three people at their cottage on Higgins Lake. They wanted me to fly over Mackinac Island. It was a beautiful day, but very windy. The guy wanted me to land on the water. I said no, because of the high winds. I could land, but may have difficulty taking off. He got upset and told me that he was going to complain to the owner. I told him, "I'm the owner."

Flights to Detroit

One day Clayton and I were pouring cement for the floor of a new hangar when a State Police car came speeding into the area where we were working. The trooper, a friend of ours, got out of the car with a young man whom we could tell had some kind of problem. Our friend informed us that his passenger's father had been injured in Detroit and was not expected to live. He wanted me to fly him to Detroit as soon as possible. I told him that I would run home and change my clothes, and then would takeoff as soon as I got back. He insisted that we takeoff right away, as every second counted.

I was in dirty old clothes, but I thought it would be a matter of dropping him off at the Detroit City Airport and that I would not even need to get out of the plane. As soon as we were airborne, he explained that he did not have any money so I would have to go to the hospital to get paid by his mother. I had no choice, but the problem was that I would have to stay overnight because I did not want to fly the Luscombe after dark.

After I received the airfare from his mother, I decided to stop in a bar and cure my thirst with a beer. A very, very large guy met me at the door and told me in no uncertain terms that the bar did not allow my type into its establishment. I had forgotten just how bad I looked.

We had a twin-engine Cessna aircraft. A couple of local ladies wanted me to fly them and their equipment to the Detroit City Airport so that they could set up a booth at Cobo Hall for a convention they were attending. When we landed, they asked me if I would help them set up the booth. I agreed. This required a long electrical extension cord to be plugged in. I proceeded to do this. A very large guy came over and informed me, in no uncertain terms, that this was his job, he was a member of the union.

This was my first experience in dealing with the union.

One day, the governor of Michigan, Governor Kim Sigler, landed in Grayling to have his brand new Bonanza aircraft refueled. He was heading for Mackinac Island to spend the weekend. I mentioned to him that the weather conditions were not good at the Island. He took me by the arm and said, "Bud, I want to show you something." He opened the door to the plane and had me look at the instrument panel. He said, "Bud, I have all the instruments required for flying in bad weather conditions." When he left, I told my brother, Clayton, about my concern for his safety. You have to know how to use those instruments. I knew. I flew in all kinds of poor weather conditions in the Pacific.

Close calls

After we purchased a twin-engine Cessna I checked Clayton out in the aircraft. A short time later, I took the afternoon off and went out to Lake Margrethe with the family to do some swimming. When I returned to the airport and drove up to the office and flight line, I noticed the Cessna was not there with the other planes (*see* Appendix A). I assumed Clayton had taken it up for a flight around the area.

When I look out on the airport, I saw that the Cessna had crashed on one of the runways. It was on its nose with the tail up in the air so I rushed out with the car and found Clayton walking around the plane. Luckily he was not injured and was quite calm about the whole thing. A mechanical malfunction

had caused the airplane to stall on takeoff when he was only a few feet in the air. If he had been much higher when it stalled, the accident would have caused him serious injury.

One day, late in the fall, I had a charter trip to fly Roy Trudegon, the owner of the Shoppegon Inn Hotel, to Iron River which is located at the western end of the Upper Peninsula (U.P.). On the way up, the weather was very bad in the U.P., and I had to fly at about 500 ft. to stay out of the low clouds. I was flying the Bellanca which was relatively fast and comfortable, but I did not like the poor flying conditions.

I told Roy that when we arrived in Iron River, I would check the weather report to see if we could fly on top of the overcast on the way back. I was told that the tops of the clouds were about 8,000 to 10,000 ft. There would be no difficulty flying "on top," and the Grayling area would remain VFR (visual flight rules). We were late departing Iron River, but we had a strong tail wind. I figured that we could still arrive back in Graying before dark where the runway lights were not working at the time.

We were doing fine, flying on top of the clouds until I estimated that we were over the straits and I received a weather report indicating that the weather in Graying and Traverse City was closing in. I had no choice but to turn back and hope to find an opening in the clouds for descending and finding a place to land. North of us in Grand Marais the ceiling was about 200 ft. with snow showers, so I decided to

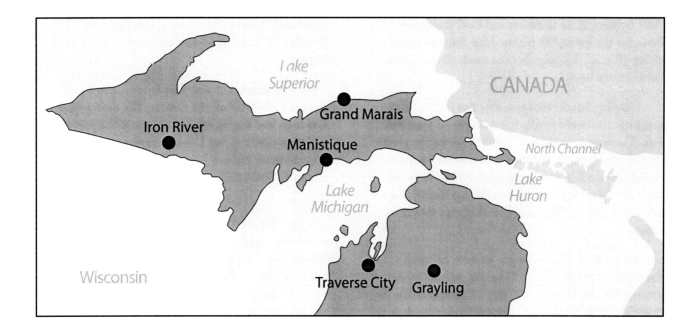

head due west and hope that I could reach Manistique to land at the airport there.

I was now flying into the strong head wind, and it was starting to get dark. I knew that Manistique's small grass field was not lighted. After anxious moments we spotted lights of a city. Although it was almost dark, I still could barely make out the airport. I descended very rapidly and landed. When I parked the plane and shut down the engine, Roy reached into his jacket and pulled out a flask. As we had a drink, I remember him saying, "that was a close one, wasn't it?" I nodded my head in the affirmative.

We went into town and got a motel room for the night, and flew back to Graying the next day.

Once in a while we drive by this airport when we are in the U.P., and I throw it a kiss.

Dawn Patrol event

In the spring, Clayton and I decided to sponsor a "dawn patrol" where pilots with light airplanes would fly in on a Sunday morning for a pancake breakfast. They would come from all over Michigan and nearby states. We received enthusiastic assistance from several local organizations with the local ladies preparing the breakfast in one of the military buildings at the airport.

In making the plans for the dawn patrol, we invited the Michigan Air National Guard with the

P-51 fighters, B-26 bombers and C-47 transports to fly in for the event. We planned for them to arrive about 10 a.m., thinking that the small planes would have arrived by then.

Grayling hardly ever gets fog, but that Sunday morning you could hardly see a couple of hundred feet. There was no control tower to advise the pilots of the small planes, and we could hear them circling on top of the fog, waiting to land. Needless to say, we were very, very worried that the fog would not lift before the Air National Guard planes would arrive.

About 9:30, the fog began to burn off and the planes started to land. Then the military planes arrived. To our amazement, they all landed safely. At that time, it was one of the largest dawn patrols to be held in Michigan.

Other parts of the business

One of my students was nearing the time when he had to solo or get "washed out" of the program. It was about his 12th hour of dual time. On a day when he had done very well with his landing and takeoff, I decided to let him solo. Most students are somewhat nervous on their first solo, but he did not appear unduly nervous when I got out of the airplane and told him to take it up for three takeoffs and landings.

His takeoff was fine, but on his base leg to his first landing, he left the throttle partially open and did not realize it. This increased his speed considerably as he was making his approach to the landing.

The runway was 6,000 ft. long and, probably to this day, he is the only pilot ot overshoot in a light airplane.

I was worried at first that he would not pull up in time at the end of the runway. His next approach was high and fast again. I could sense the panic he was experiencing, but I could do nothing about it because we did not have two-way radios in that airplane. Nevertheless, he did finally land the plane okay.

By 1951 we had trained most of the veterans who were interested in getting their private pilot's license. We were getting some charter flights and had become a dealer for Onan Electric Generator Plant to give us much needed income. After a few years, the business would not support two families, so I moved to Battle Creek, Michigan, and in 1953 I was called back into the Marine Corps for the Korean War.

8
THE KOREAN WAR

Just before Christmas in December 1952, the Marine Corps called me back as a Captain for the Korean War. I reported to the Marine Corps Air Station at Cherry Point, North Carolina, and was assigned to a Marine Air Group consisting of three jet-fighter aircraft squadrons.

My ground job was Assistant Communication Officer, placed in charge of the secret and confidential files and codes. Passenger flights included trips to Boston, Norfolk, Washington, D.C., Miami, Jacksonville, Cuba, Jamaica, Detroit, Puerto Rico, and the Virgin Islands. I also obtained a few hours of flight time in a jet.

R5D Marine Transport in Korea

R5D cockpit

British C-47 and P-51
aircraft, Korea

Back Out West

Later I was transferred to the Marine Corps Air Station at El Toro, California, to become a plane commander on the four- engine R5D transport that carried about 50 passengers. Further transfers were to naval air stations in Corpus Christi, Texas, and Barbers Point, Hawaii.

Our Maintenance Squadron was based at Barber's Point in Oahu, Hawaii. At Barbers Point I was assigned to a Marine Air Transport Squadron that was part of a forward unit stationed at Iwakuni, Japan (near Hiroshima). We would spend about three weeks in Japan, flying troops in and out of Korea, and then rotate back to Hawaii for about ten days of repairs. My family was able to join me in Hawaii. Joyce and our son, Doug, who was about four years old, had a good time going to the swimming beach and seeing the sights.

Korean Terrain and Bad Weather

Korean was very hilly and mountainous. Flights to Korea were therefore sometimes very difficult because of it. One airfield called K-3 had a hill near the runway that we had to fly over when landing. The operator's job was keeping us on the glide path to a landing.

When approaching K-3 we would try to stay above the glide path because of the hill which we could not see. In bad weather (poor visibility and low ceilings), we had to land using GCA (Ground Control Approach) radar. As a plane commander with a "Green Card," I was authorized to land with ceilings of a minimum of 200 feet and one-quarter mile visibility. Then we were flying on instruments and knew the hill was there. When passing the hill, the operator would say, "Okay, Marine 9999, you can let down now. You are over the hill."

Japaneese alley

Routine Flight Duty

We had a daily night trip to Tokyo and occasional flights to Hong Kong. After the tour we would fly back to Hawaii via Midway Island, at 30° latitude just east of the International Date Line. The trip to Midway from Tokyo was our longest trip over the Pacific, about 2300 miles. A week or so later we would rotate back to Japan via the southern route with stops at the islands of Kwajalein and Guam.

Destination Hong Kong

When I was stationed in Japan, one day we were assigned to a flight to Hong Kong, China. This was a surprise as we had not been to Hong Kong before, and it was an extended flight for us.

At the time, the communists controlled China, but the British still occupied Hong Kong. We were very apprehensive. About 200 miles out, we called the tower and requested landing information. They gave us the runway to use and other required information. As we approached the runway, we noticed there was vehicle traffic crossing the runway.

We informed the tower about our concern, and they radioed back, "DON'T WORRY OLD BOY, WE WILL HAVE THE TRAFFIC STOPPED BEFORE YOU LAND!" A street crossed the runway and barriers were extended to stop the traffic when an aircraft was on its final approach to the landing.

Hong Kong, British Crown Colony, airfield

Home for Good

Early 1955 saw me back at El Toro, and on July 1, 1955, I was discharged from the Marine Corps.

A street scene in China

The Coaster based in Traverse City

9
POST-WAR LIFE

In 1955, the war had ended and I was ready to make a change. I was offered a pilot's job with Pan American Airlines and would be based in New York City, making flights to England and Europe. This would mean living in New York. This did not appeal to Joyce and me, so we decided to move to Traverse City, Michigan.

Being a captain, I received a pretty good salary, and as a pilot, I received a monthly bonus for flight duty. We had saved enough money to provide adequate funds for the expenses and adjustment to a civilian life if we couldn't find a job right away.

Traverse City

I met and formed a partnership with Jack Zimmerman, who was the leading residential builder who owned a construction company. I had to start Zimmerman-McDonnell Realty Company from scratch because I did not know anyone nor was I familiar with Traverse City. Over the years I grew the company into 18 sales people in the residential department and five in the commercial department, becoming the Realtor of the Year in both 1961 and 1977. In 1977 I was also president of the Board of Realtors, while staying active in the Chamber of Commerce for many years. I also formed some investment groups.

Having divorced by this time, in the early 1970s I remarried. Honey Ward was a U.P. native who had been born in Hancock, Michigan. While in Traverse City, Honey and I did a lot of boating in our 40-ft. cruiser and toured Lake Superior along its northern Canadian shore. I loved to boat and fish, and we ended up owning a nice home on East Bay with a boat out in front. My sons, Doug and Gary, had good schools, and we all enjoyed living there (*see* Appendix B).

The Coaster

Our 40-ft. trawler had two diesel engines, a steel hull, and was equipped with radar. It was custom built for a Grayling friend of mine who was living in Houghton in the U.P. When we purchased the boat, we made the trip to Traverse City where we lived at that time. From Houghton our first stop was Isle Royale for a few days, before many stops along Lake Superior, Lake Huron, and Lake Michigan.

Along the south shore of Canada we mainly stayed in small bays as there were few marinas and cities. One night when we were anchored in a small

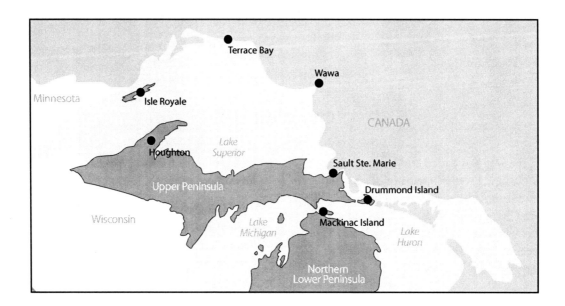

bay, a very strong wind came up. I worried about the anchor holding, as we were very near the shore behind us. Fortunately the boat had a search light and I could focus it on a nearby tree to see if we were being blown towards the shore. That storm lasted about three hours.

One time in the middle of Lake Superior about 40 Monarch butterflies landed on the boat for a rest stop. We were told later that they were on their way to Mexico for the winter, a real mystery to us that they could travel that distance.

We went through the Soo Locks. Then to the North Channel in Canada, then to Drummond Island, Mackinac Island, Mackinaw City, then home to Traverse City. This trip took about a month, and it was quite an adventure for Honey and me.

After that we made many trips to Northport, Charlevoix, Harbor Springs, Beaver Island, South Manitou Island and Leland.

A Bit of Migration

In 1980–82 interest rates went up to 20% and financing of all kinds was hard to get. I had to sell Zimmerman-McDonnell. We moved to Ft. Collins, Colorado, where we lived for two years,. However, the economy was real bad and we wanted to return to Michigan.

Because I knew a commercial realtor in Kalamazoo, we chose this community, moved, and stayed. We've been comfortable here for 20 years already.

10
LOOKING BACK

I recently became aware of how fortunate I was in taking the exam to enter the Naval Aviation Cadet Program to learn to be a Marine pilot. Number one, I would not have had the qualifications and money to start the Grayling Air Service. Number two, I would not have had the funds for our living expenses and investment in Zimmerman-McDonnell Realty Company. Traverse City was the right choice for us in the mid-1950s.

In many ways, it does not seem like this all happened over nearly the last 70 years. As a plane commander in both WWII and Korea, I was expected to fly in all kinds of weather. When crews were on instruments, we often flew into thunderstorms because we had no airborne radar to warn us. We would be brought into a landing by radar (GCA , Ground Control Approach). You had to have a lot of faith in the controller.

When I look back on the tremendous responsibility young pilots had at the age of 22, plus the war-time experience, it had was quite awesome. We carried about 35 Marine passengers (many times, high-ranking Marines) over thousands of miles of the Pacific Ocean into war zones. How many times did I brief them prior to takeoff? Their thoughts must have included, "Am I putting my life into the hands of crazy youth who think they're immortal?" But they did not have the choice of getting off the plane and requesting their money back.

My memories are still very clear of being a Marine pilot flying a twin-engine transport and being stationed on the Island of Guam in 1944 and 1945, with involvement in many of the Marine battles in the Pacific. On the 50th anniversaries of the 1945 Iwo Jima and Okinawa invasions, I was invited to speak at the Kalamazoo Air Zoo which presented me with the 1995 Spirit of Flight Award in the Michigan Aviation Hall of Fame (see Appendix C).

Souvenirs that I might have kept are not that important to me now, and I have given my gold aviation wings to my son Doug because he wanted them. Doug and I have been quite active at the Air Zoo. He spent a lot of time being a guide and advisor at the original building.

There was a "plus side" to WWII. The economy improved compared to that of the 1930s. Many of my friends were able to go to college on the G.I. Bill. My brother and I were able to purchase three training planes from a bank using the G.I. Bill to start the Grayling Air Service, and I purchased my first home for $21,000 using the Veterans Home Loan program.

Now I am 90 years young, still interested in the world around me and as physically active as possible. I love cross-country skiing in the arboretum near my home. Healthful exercise and community engagement will do well to keep younger people happy throughout their lifetimes too.

Grandpa Bud with Anna, son Gary's daughter

APPENDIX A
Aircraft Owned by Grayling Air Service

3 Luscombes | Our training planes were two-place with side-by-side seating and 65-horsepower engines. They cruised about 100 mph.

1 PT-19 | A war-surplus, acrobatic training plane with a single in-line engine of 200 horsepower.

1 Seabee | This four-place amphibian seaplane cruised about 115 mph. I had a lot of fun with this airplane, taking charter trips to Drummond Island to fish. We only charged $18 per person (three people max) for airfare, overnight lodging, and a boat with motor to fish within the bays.

1 Bellanca | Another four-place, low-wing aircraft with retractable landing gear which cruised about 150 mph. We used this plane for charter trips, and it was the only plane that did not depreciate. We paid $3,500 for it and used the plane for about two years before selling it to a doctor near Lansing for $3,500.

1 Cessna | A war-surplus plane, purchased to train veterans for twin-engine ratings.

Doug McDonnell in front of Bud's Mooney airplane in Traverse City

APPENDIX B
Family Recreation

My two sons, Gary and Doug, were both interested in aviation. Every year we attended the air meet, the Fly-In, in Oshkosh, Wisconsin. In the winter we would cross-country ski in the Glen Lake area in Leelanau County and near Traverse City.

Bud (right) with his sons, Gary (left) and Doug (center)

Michigan Aviation Hall of Fame

1995 Spirit of Flight Award

all Michigan Aviation Pioneers who served in World war II.

Bud McDonnell

represents all Michigan Citizens who served in
Marine Air Service during WW II

APPENDIX C
Aviation Hall of Fame

This award waspresented in 1995 after I spoke at the Kalamazoo Air Zoo twice in celebrations of the invasions of Iwo Jima and Okinawa.

A B-25 bomber visits Kalamazoo in July 2013

INDEX

NOTE: The italic letter p following a page number indicates that the subject information of the heading is pictured on that page. A double italic pp means more than one illustration per page.

CPSIA information can be obtained at www.ICGtesting.com
Printed in the USA
BVOW02s0620281013

334816BV00002B/4/P